The Earth's Surface

Illustrated by Ute Fuhr and Raoul Sautai
Created by Gallimard Jeunesse

MOONLIGHT PUBLISHING / FIRST DISCOVERY

What is geography really for?

Seen from space, the Earth is a blue planet.

To get to know
what the surface of the Earth looks like.

It is blue because oceans and seas cover two thirds of its surface.
The rest is taken up by the continents.

From an aeroplane, the surface of the Earth appears to be made of peaks, bumps, hollows and great flat stretches of land with rivers flowing through them.

The coastline can be rocky and uneven…

Peninsula

Point

Beach

Cove

Island

Islet

Inlet

Bay

... or else flat and sandy.

Sandbank

Dune

A Norwegian fjord

Along Bay in Vietnam

Coastlines vary from continent to continent and from country to country.

Chalk cliffs

A tropical mangrove

A tropical beach

A sandy coastline
surrounded by coral reefs

High mountains have pointed tops: they are called peaks.

Glacier

Permanent snow field

Pass

Lake

Waterfall

Torrent

Down below are valleys with rivers flowing down them.

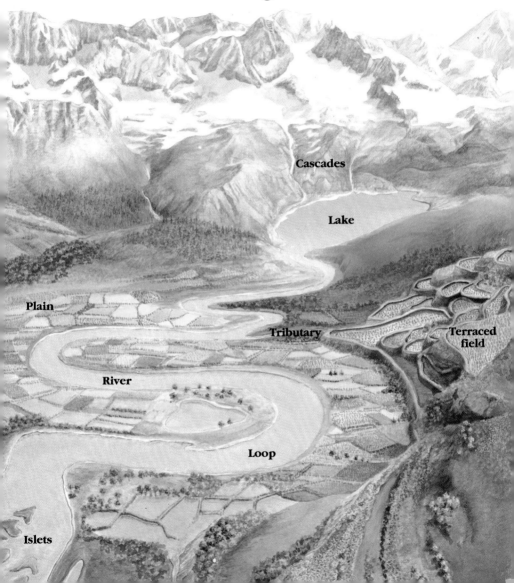

Cascades

Lake

Plain

Tributary

Terraced field

River

Loop

Islets

Mount Everest
in the Himalayas

The Olga Mountains
in Australia

Machu Picchu
in Peru

Over time the weather, the cold, the winds, the rain
and the river waters…

The Sea of Ice in the Alps

A vast plain in the American Far West

... change the landscape.

The Ganges Delta in India

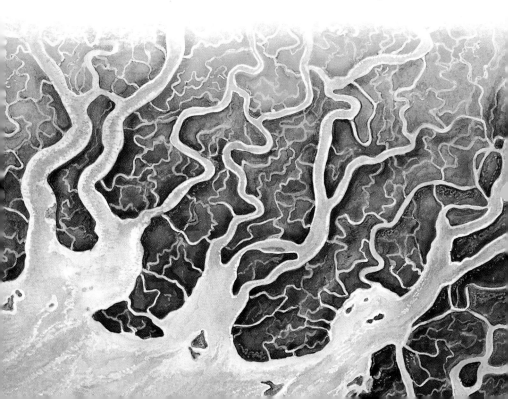

The Colorado River has little by little dug out
a very narrow, very deep valley
in the soft rock.

Today it has become the famous Grand Canyon.

Volcanic eruptions change the landscape completely
Mountains take on a new shape...

... new islands
come up out of
the sea

A forest of the Far North

Very cold and very hot climates...

Ice flow

Iceberg

A savanna

An equatorial forest

... create unusual landscapes.

A desert

An inselberg, the remains
of an eroded mountain

Only a century ago, the countryside was still in its natural state.

Plateau

Natural lake

Fields

Confluence

Marshland

Meadows surrounded
by natural hedges

Today we have changed landscapes everywhere: motorways, bridges, factories, towns, dams...

Dish antennae

Wind turbines

Village

Artificial lake

Bridge

Deforested area

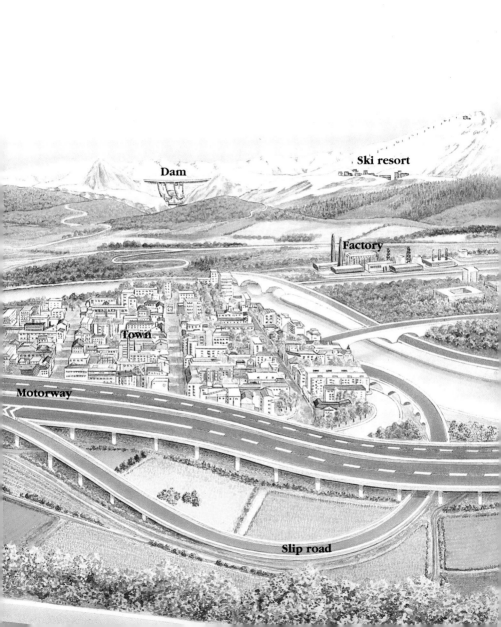

Dam

Ski resort

Factory

Town

Motorway

Slip road

FIRST DISCOVERY: OVER 125 TITLES AVAILABLE IN 5 SERIES

American Indians
Animal Camouflage
Animals in Danger
Babies
Bears
The Beaver
The Bee
Being Born
Birds
Boats
The Body
The Building Site
The Butterfly
The Castle
Cathedrals
Cats
Christmas and New Year
Clothes and Costumes
Colours
Counting
The Crocodile
The Desert
Dinosaurs
Dogs
Ducks
The Eagle
Earth and Sky
The Earth's Surface
The Egg
The Elephant
Farm Animals
Finding a Mate
Firefighting
Flowers
Flying
Football
The Frog
Fruit
Growing Up
Halloween
The Hedgehog
Homes

The Horse
How the Body Works
The Internet
The Jungle
The Ladybird
Light
The Lion
Monkeys and Apes
Mountains
The Mouse
Music
On Wheels
The Owl
Penguins
Pictures
Pirates
Prehistoric People
Pyramids
Rabbits
The Riverbank
The Seashore
Shapes
Shops
Small Animals in the Home
Sport
The Story of Bread
The Telephone
The Tiger
Time
Town
Trains
The Tree
Under the Ground
Up and Down
Vegetables
Volcanoes
Water
The Weather
Whales
The Wind
The Wolf

FIRST DISCOVERY / ATLAS
Animal Atlas
Atlas of Animals in Danger
Atlas of Civilizations
Atlas of Countries
Atlas of the Earth
Atlas of France
Atlas of Islands
Atlas of Peoples
Atlas of Space
Plant Atlas

FIRST DISCOVERY / ART
Animals
Henri Matisse
The Impressionists
Landscapes
The Louvre
Pablo Picasso
Paintings
Paul Gauguin
Portraits
Sculpture
Vincent van Gogh

FIRST DISCOVERY / TORCHLIGHT
Let's Look at Animals by Night
Let's Look at Animals Underground
Let's Look at Archimboldo's Portraits
Let's Look at Castles
Let's Look at Caves
Let's Look at Dinosaurs
Let's Look at Faires, Witches, Giants and Dragons
Let's Look at Fish Underwater
Let's Look at Life below the City
Let's Look at Insects
Let's Look inside the Body
Let's Look at the Jungle
Let's Look at the Sky
Let's Look at the Zoo by Night
Let's Look for Lost Treasure
Let's Look inside Pyramids
Let's Look for Lost Treasure

FIRST DISCOVERY CLOSE-UPS
Let's Look at the Garden close up
Let's Look at the Hedge close up
Let's Look at the Oak close up
Let's Look at the Pond close up
Let's Look at the Rainforest close up
Let's Look at the Seashore close up
Let's Look at the Stream close up
Let's Look at the Vegetable Garden close
Let's Look under the Stone close up

Translator: Penelope Stanley-Baker
ISBN 1 85103362 9
© 2004 by Editions Gallimard Jeunesse
English text © 2005 by Moonlight Publishing Ltd
First published in the United Kingdom 2005
by Moonlight Publishing Limited, The King's Manor, East Hendred, Oxon. OX12 8JY
Printed in Italy by Editoriale Lloyd

[13]